About the Author

Jessica Elaine is an Australian poet, heavily influenced by intimate experience. Her work comprises short impactful moments, cascading with raw emotion and captivating the mind through deepened thought.

"There can be no social shame when we are universally connected through the privacy of words on a page."
- Jessica Elaine

The L Collection

Jessica Elaine

The L Collection

Olympia Publishers
London

www.olympiapublishers.com
OLYMPIA PAPERBACK EDITION

Copyright © Jessica Elaine 2023

The right of Jessica Elaine to be identified as author of
this work has been asserted in accordance with sections 77 and 78 of
the Copyright, Designs and Patents Act 1988.

All Rights Reserved

No reproduction, copy or transmission of this publication
may be made without written permission.
No paragraph of this publication may be reproduced,
copied or transmitted save with the written permission of the publisher,
or in accordance with the provisions
of the Copyright Act 1956 (as amended).

Any person who commits any unauthorised act in relation to
this publication may be liable to criminal
prosecution and civil claims for damage.

A CIP catalogue record for this title is
available from the British Library.

ISBN: 978-1-80074-722-7

First Published in 2023

Olympia Publishers
Tallis House
2 Tallis Street
London
EC4Y 0AB

Printed in Great Britain

Dedication

I dedicate this collection to those who seize opportunity,
navigating forward into the unknown.
And to Marcus.
Our Empire, unbreakable.

Acknowledgements

To Olympia Publishers, who saw my life through words on a page and felt it deserving of a chance to reach the world.

PART ONE
LOVE

You are a story worthy of being told.

– Jessica Elaine

It is simply infecting.
To know that with you I am the version of myself I aspire to be.
And you instil passion, a desire to grow.

– Jessica Elaine

When I think that I am done and have articulated all that I can, my mind conjures more.
Because the simple truth is, I can never get enough of you.

— Jessica Elaine

As of late I have come to realize my expectation has been altered.
Because I cannot give up on you so quickly.
And because you deserve my attention.

— Jessica Elaine

I thrive off of you.
And you bring out the most exciting parts buried within.
And you have made me feel.

– Jessica Elaine

You are the adventure I have always desired.

— Jessica Elaine

You filled me with a fantasy so vivid that reality can no longer compare. And I consider that to live in this state of mind provides a satisfaction so grand, it may be all I need.

– Jessica Elaine

My roots have become entangled, as I lose myself deep within you.

— Jessica Elaine

Indulge me, if only for a night.

— Jessica Elaine

Our physical chemistry undeniable as my body dissolves into submission at your touch.
But the most intense experience with you is our intellectual connection.
Relishing in hours the depth of your mind takes me.

– Jessica Elaine

Nothing more than a fleeting encounter and you have
bewitched my thoughts.
Leaving only hope that we will in fact meet again.

– Jessica Elaine

It is simply uncontrollable.
How I am thrust into a state of submission.
And I am artlessly bound to you in ways I cannot comprehend.

— Jessica Elaine

An ability to mesmerize me through your voice and my body to grow weak at your touch.

— Jessica Elaine

I am incapable of loving anything in the capacity to which I love you.

– Jessica Elaine

I feel a pleasure from your voice and I am left satisfied by your company.

— Jessica Elaine

It was you who showed me that in fact love can be unconditional.

– Jessica Elaine

You have poured a perception of life over me and I know simply that I am grateful for you.

— Jessica Elaine

I am intoxicated simply by your presence.

— Jessica Elaine

With me, there are no boundaries on what you can dream.
And I will dream beside you.

– Jessica Elaine

The weight of insecurity renders me speechless as I remain paralyzed by the simple fact, that I have never met anyone like you before.

– Jessica Elaine

And before anything else it was your mind I fell in love with.
How you make me think and how I view the world through
new eyes.

— Jessica Elaine

You ignited a dream within me so grand that I cannot remember a time when passion oozed from me this fiercely.

– Jessica Elaine

And for now, all I can do is dream of you and long for the day when you are near.

– Jessica Elaine

It is a simple dream.
Where you love me and I am happy.

— Jessica Elaine

And if the sun does not rise tomorrow, I need you to know
that I love you.
And that I have always loved you.

– Jessica Elaine

I had a dream.
And you were there. And you loved me.

– Jessica Elaine

And if you can glimpse beyond the noise, you will find that I am in fact still in love with you.

– Jessica Elaine

A memory of you burnt so deep within I can feel you near.
And I am longing for your touch.
And searching for your voice behind closed eyes.

– Jessica Elaine

How was I to know that I was capable of feeling this way, of needing anyone other than myself.
But you ignited a spark within me that burnt out long ago.

– Jessica Elaine

I am only capable of loving completely and with depth.

— Jessica Elaine

I awake beside you absorbing a feeling of contentment and realize that this is what I have always wanted.

– Jessica Elaine

You are a constant light cascading over me.
Bringing purpose and brightening life.

— Jessica Elaine

After all these years I remain humbled that you are mine.
An endless supply of love, filtering through my life.

— Jessica Elaine

But no matter what happens, there will always be a piece of me that belongs only to you.

— Jessica Elaine

How can I ever be satisfied with anything else now that I have known you?

— Jessica Elaine

Meet me in my dreams.
Where the weight of the world's problems no longer exist,
and where we can kiss without judgement.

— Jessica Elaine

My mind is constantly active.
Learning. Thinking. Creating.
Stimulate that more than my body and I am yours.

– Jessica Elaine

I would rather walk through life with this painful burning accompanying my soul than to be anything but yours.

— Jessica Elaine

I am weakened by the mere thought of you.
Paralyzing my mind, burning into my soul. Leaving invisible scars across my heart.

— Jessica Elaine

Take me on a journey.
Entwine your hands within mine and together create a life we never imagined possible.

– Jessica Elaine

And after this considerable measure of time, I am still inspired by you. Consuming life with purpose. Sealing the gap of insecurity and self-doubt.

— Jessica Elaine

Your kiss is stained upon my lips for eternity.
And there it will remain waiting, for the day you return.

– Jessica Elaine

How do I close my heart to the considerable amount of love I have built for you?
The sweet sound of your voice embedded in my ears, or the intoxicating scent you leave behind.
How does your touch cease to burn my skin?
Or the closing of my eyes to fantasies that you are in fact the one.

– Jessica Elaine

A mere moment of looking into your eyes,
they have become stained within my memory and your voice
ringing through my ears.
I search, but cannot find you.
Appearing among vivid dreams so repetitive I am torn
between sleep and awake.

– Jessica Elaine

In the darkness your silhouette is ever present.
My eyes close to the invisible touch you place upon my back
and breath as your lips brush across my neck.
My fingers grasp loose sheets as your scent continues to
linger throughout and your voice echoes within my mind.

– Jessica Elaine

Finally, as though my entire life were leading to this moment,
I am here.
And all I can see is you and a love so deep,
to lose it would be to lose myself.

– Jessica Elaine

A life now brimming with meaning.
You have restored love to a broken soul and ignited light
into dark corners of my being.
A love so deep my roots are embedded in a lifetime of
loving you.

– Jessica Elaine

Infecting my dreams with a face I am yet to meet.
Thoughts drifting into a fantasy of who you are.
Consuming my mind so intensely, I am willing you to life.

– Jessica Elaine

What I feel is a belonging to you.
That my being sought through a galaxy of trauma and experience and at the end, there you were.
And I cannot consciously exist without you.

— Jessica Elaine

And when you need me, I will come.
Subconsciously I am already there.

– Jessica Elaine

The memory of our first encounter so prominent in my
mind.
My world shifting into a state a bliss,
and I began to burn again.
You flamed life into me merely by your ability to live
and I crave to feel your sense of freedom.

— Jessica Elaine

I glanced at the wall you had built about yourself, not an ounce of intimidation.
And the higher you build, the higher I climb.
And when you push me away, I will return.

— Jessica Elaine

And I am broken by the realization that because of you, nothing will ever be enough.

– Jessica Elaine

I struggle to articulate.
But what I have determined is that he is utterly out of his mind.
And with every passing moment, I am falling in love.

– Jessica Elaine

I cannot be satisfied knowing that my love is wasted.
And I have to wonder if I can live a life without you.

– Jessica Elaine

I am aware now that it is not enough.
Because I want more.
I want all of you and to love only you.

– Jessica Elaine

And when you arrived the rain stopped and the skies cleared.
Sun lighting a life before me that I was unable to see.
And the internal suffering ceased.

– Jessica Elaine

I remain entranced simply by your presence and you are a constant thief of my thoughts.

— Jessica Elaine

You have dissolved the defences that once surrounded me.
Restoring desire to an otherwise hopeless soul.

– Jessica Elaine

And what remains are indulgent memories, a chapter of my life worthy of remaining in the forefront of my mind.

– Jessica Elaine

Do not flatter yourself, for it is easy to get into my heart. But to explore the labyrinth of my mind and reside there is a rarity.

– Jessica Elaine

I can only hope to provide a love so unconditional that the invisible scars existing within your soul dissolve and you are exposed to a life you became afraid to dream of.

– Jessica Elaine

As silence of night engulfs empty space around you, I wonder selfishly if I am in your thoughts.

– Jessica Elaine

Where you are going, I will be there.

– Jessica Elaine

I accidentally fell in love with you.
Captivated by your perception of the world.

– Jessica Elaine

Take me into the depths of your mind.
And let me reside there to feast on all that you are.

— Jessica Elaine

To be in your presence surrounded by silence, I would continue to remain engrossed by you.

– Jessica Elaine

He was a blessing.
Invigorating souls he encountered.

– Jessica Elaine

I cannot fathom the span of time that has passed since I was last weighted by your body.

— Jessica Elaine

Exhaust my mind in conversation and my body through your touch.

– Jessica Elaine

It is simply unimaginable, the ways in which you distract me.

— Jessica Elaine

Behind closed eyes, I am never far away.

— Jessica Elaine

There will always be a place under my arm when you require safety.
And time will have no restrictions.

– Jessica Elaine

I gazed over his external beauty, savouring the way my body involuntarily reacted.
And then he exposed his mind.
And I am constantly drowning in his perception of the world around him.

– Jessica Elaine

An obsessive desire to consume myself with thoughts of only you.
And to willingly drown in the sound of your voice as you whisper in my ear.

– Jessica Elaine

There is no denying, for I have drowned in you completely.

– Jessica Elaine

My desire for you is indescribable as I am wrenched from reality into the unknown.

– Jessica Elaine

A love so unconditional I have forgotten life without it.
And I cannot fathom a time where you did not exist and
where I was not whole.

– Jessica Elaine

And in your absence, I remain satisfied by the memories that permanently reside within my mind.

— Jessica Elaine

There will be no hesitation to reassure you, I am only yours.

— Jessica Elaine

You have transformed fantasy into reality.

– Jessica Elaine

PART TWO
LOSS

A mere moment of looking into your eyes,
they have become stained within my memory and your voice
ringing through my ears.
I search, but cannot find you.
Appearing among vivid dreams so repetitive I am torn
between sleep and awake.

– Jessica Elaine

It is not a painful wait.
And know that when you return, I will still be here.

– Jessica Elaine

Your touch burnt so deeply against my skin.
A permanent memory remaining, never to fade.

– Jessica Elaine

I yearn for the nights where I lost myself within your stories.
And where I fell asleep to the sound of your breath.

– Jessica Elaine

On occasion my thoughts betray me, diverting to you.
And I drift between memory and fantasy.

– Jessica Elaine

I was your willing puppet, unable to detach.
Remaining exhausted on the ends of your strings, bound
between controlling fingers.

– Jessica Elaine

There can be no measure to what I would have given, for you to occupy this space beside me.

– Jessica Elaine

As the pages of life turn you will fade from memory,
the desire diminishing.
And you slid away ever so gently,
becoming a stranger once more.

– Jessica Elaine

I believed that my ability to trust unconditionally
was my downfall.
But I have learnt that this character trait is not my fault,
rather yours, the one who abused it.

– Jessica Elaine

Do not misunderstand my commitment following the aftermath of your destruction as weakness. Rather, reflect that my consistency exists because of my investment in you.

– Jessica Elaine

I must thank you for instantaneously providing a beginning, middle and end.
For I was indescribably restrained to you.

– Jessica Elaine

Liberated by the idea that when I have healed from the agony you have placed upon me, I will no longer feel burden.

– Jessica Elaine

As I grapple with the fallout from our reckless encounter
I am left to consider.
Perhaps you were the lesson, not the outcome.

– Jessica Elaine

I am submerged in questions you left behind.
Drowning without closure.

– Jessica Elaine

I spend hours being consumed by you.
You appear in the books I read, the songs I hear
and the people I see.
Take me with you for I cannot fathom that you are
no longer with me.

– Jessica Elaine

I have come to realize that there is nothing you owe me and that I am of no obligation to you.
And I choose to no longer tolerate being an option, when you are always my choice.

– Jessica Elaine

In an endless cycle of disappointment, I am exhausted.
And I was willing, my desire for you unmeasurable.

– Jessica Elaine

And in an instant, it all changed.
And I am no longer on the border of your presence
as I refuse to let my worth be shadowed by your
inability to see me.

– Jessica Elaine

You poisoned me, infecting my life.
And when I see you, I see nothingness.
And I starved my time by loving you.

– Jessica Elaine

No pleasure can be found in your vague responses.
And my worth is far greater than what you attempt to give.

– Jessica Elaine

I yearn to return home.
Where my heart was full and where I felt love.

— Jessica Elaine

It is as though I wake up in the dark, every day.
I am here but I am not present and my heart aches for you.

— Jessica Elaine

A deep feeling of hope burning thin.
And there is no relief from the pain in a cycle of continual hurt.
And I am left to wonder when it will stop or
when I will stop.

— Jessica Elaine

I grow weary of your apologies and attempts of self-improvement.

– Jessica Elaine

As night closes out the day I crawl into a bed of uncertainty. A blanket of anxiety weighs on top of me and I am left to wonder if tomorrow will come.

— Jessica Elaine

And in the face of real tragedy, we are forced to recognize
the value of life.
And to be grateful.
And to be present.

– Jessica Elaine

A dark sky now setting above us.
An unfathomable pain and what remains is a sea of tears the world has cried for you.

– Jessica Elaine

Have you found the peace you sought?
An unbearable pain remains but I will take comfort in
knowing you are free from the evil within.
Unaware of your suffering.
Thoughts drifting around and I wonder if the light that took
you was pure comfort?
You can rest now.

— Jessica Elaine

A loss so painful a piece of the soul can never repair.

– Jessica Elaine

I am constrained to a loop.
A never-ending cycle of uncertainty.

– Jessica Elaine

You may be gone my love but for as long as the universe continues to expand, my heart will forever beat alongside the memory of your voice and behind closed eyes I will see you staring back at me.

– Jessica Elaine

I am sitting in the middle of a ship; it has a hole.
Water consuming the space around me and I am sinking.
Not fast, but slow.
Watching everything around me disappear.

– Jessica Elaine

I am in love with the idea of freedom.
Released from the depths the mind chooses to wander without control.
I am chained down by my mind, unable to find the key to unlock it.
I am yet to find freedom.

– Jessica Elaine

I wear a mask routinely.
What does my mask look like to those who see
what I cannot?
My own reflection reveals self-revulsion.
I see invisible chains consuming my wrists, ankles and
securely around my throat.
The lock binding the chains are unable to be loosened as my
mind forces them to remain there.

– Jessica Elaine

I long for a day where leaving the confines of my own mind no longer torment me.

– Jessica Elaine

And what remains are invisible scars across my heart from a life so lonely, that even the voices in my head despise me.

– Jessica Elaine

And then there was darkness.
No noise surrounding me, no taste in food, no substance in conversation.
Just like that, you were gone.

– Jessica Elaine

The intensity of self-doubt weighs enormous pressure on the mind.
Drowning amongst your own thoughts and clutching onto an invisible safety line.

— Jessica Elaine

And it was so easy for you to say goodbye.
Your words like poison, paralyzing.
A soul now in oblivion.

— Jessica Elaine

As dark clouds roll in shadowing the light in my mind, thoughts grasp onto an invisible safety line and I am reminded that there is always hope.

– Jessica Elaine

Carelessly, I torment myself with the thought that your life now cascades with all I was unable to give.

– Jessica Elaine

Chaos in the confines of my mind.
Never ending, conflicting.
The immense pressure gives as I fall, drowning in a sea of voices that surround me.

– Jessica Elaine

A dark shadow persists to weight over me.
I am sinking underneath the enormity of pressure
and consumed with the fear that this time I may not be able
to get back up.

– Jessica Elaine

My body keeps going but my head moves further away from reality.
I am grasping onto the internal voice whispering that tomorrow will be better.

— Jessica Elaine

My life, represented through a bucket supporting a hairline split, resting below a dripping tap.
Efforts observed, relishing in the rise as pages of my life turn.
But somehow left defeated by the slow disappearance.
Examining for error, longing to know if the bucket will become full and if I will ever feel complete.

– Jessica Elaine

Life is quiet now. And I just miss you.

— Jessica Elaine

I sit idly by, hoping that one day I will be enough.

– Jessica Elaine

You are not tied to this life alongside me.
So I propose if you no longer desire to stay, leave.
Because I want you, I do not need you.

— Jessica Elaine

PART THREE
LIFE

My empire is built on love and the choice to self-sacrifice.

– Jessica Elaine

Consider that fulfilment can be found within the simplicities of life.
Ease in conversation, burning through a touch.

– Jessica Elaine

Unexpectedly, the seed once planted and forgotten grew into something so unimaginable that the perception of the world was instantly changed.
And it was in that moment that the understanding of patience had come to fruition.

– Jessica Elaine

And I come to realize just how unconditional my love can be and remain focused on the concept that this is what drives me forward.

— Jessica Elaine

And I choose to seize this opportunity.
Carrying thoughts of strength as I navigate forward into the unknown.

– Jessica Elaine

I like to think that I have experienced this pain with the challenge to survive in order to be worthy of love.

– Jessica Elaine

There can be no social shame when we are universally connected through words on page.

— Jessica Elaine

As darkness oozes its way into the mind we are drowned by its presence.
Only those with strength and persistence will look within to find a mere glimpse of light at the end.

— Jessica Elaine

I feel as though I am a passenger of life.
I sit and observe change and evolution around me yet I am
unable to progress as others do.
The weight of self-doubt keeps me seated.

– Jessica Elaine

An unknown feeling consumes my mind as I work
to find its resolve.
And I come to the realization that perhaps this is something
I have not experienced before, but have always wanted.

– Jessica Elaine

As though awakened from darkness, uncertainty of the future is no longer haunting.
Rather I have chosen to find adventure, pathed by the unknown of every day.

– Jessica Elaine

My perception is now in question as you have illustrated the simplicity of life.

– Jessica Elaine

You have brought a sense of realism to life.
A true understanding of creating something you yourself
would desire, even if you are alone.

– Jessica Elaine

As I sit and wander through the depths of my mind, you are the only thing that remains constant.
A reassurance, that loyalty does exist.

– Jessica Elaine

Understand that it is not the responsibility of others to create your happiness.

– Jessica Elaine

It is an arduous task to find the truth, when from the mouths of many such nonsense is spilled.

– Jessica Elaine

I once read a book so grand that I did not want it to end.
And as though a realization occurred, I compared the similarities between the act of finishing the book and life itself.
And I no longer fear the end, rather embracing life as though they are chapters.
And the end of life is to simply finish the last chapter and close the book.

— Jessica Elaine

As waves lapped against the shoreline my mind was at peace.
And in the vast distance, I finally saw hope.

— Jessica Elaine

I will plant an idea in the ground and provide a foundation so strong that no matter the wind change it will be indestructible.

– Jessica Elaine

When all hope seems lost and I have sunken to the darkest places of my mind you appear.
Without question, without hesitation and bring me back to life.

– Jessica Elaine

My mind searches for answers in a world full of questions.

– Jessica Elaine

Clarity in moments ensure our future is carved with purpose and self-improvement.

– Jessica Elaine

Be your own light in a world so dark.

– Jessica Elaine

And in the midst of the chaos there always remains hope.

– Jessica Elaine

And along the journey of life the realization becomes more prominent that there is in fact an end.

— Jessica Elaine

The uncertainty of what's to come next leaves a frightening realization within, and I am left to consider that the unknown is more of an adventure than I have ever had.

– Jessica Elaine

I once sat under the night sky realizing the vast space that surrounded me, and suddenly my uncertainties seemed insignificant.

– Jessica Elaine

Nothing more than a heartbeat from within and I am already in love with you.

— Jessica Elaine

Sometimes in our darkest hour someone can bring meaning to life.
And the sadness dissolves.
And what remains is a feeling of peace.

– Jessica Elaine

Sometimes you read in a strangers face their suffering and feel so helpless to provide comfort.

— Jessica Elaine

I came to the city seeking answers but instead have discovered only unanswerable questions.

– Jessica Elaine

The sun setting in the distance.
Warmth dissipating along with orange and pink tones,
and I close my eyes and fill my thoughts with gratitude.

– Jessica Elaine

Maybe this wasn't a tragedy but a lesson.
To show us strength, kindness.
To teach selflessness.
And maybe from this, we will understand the act of giving and to be grateful.

— Jessica Elaine

I once fell apart so completely, the rebuild was simply magnificent.

– Jessica Elaine

PART FOUR
LABYRINTH

The darkness of night consuming the space around me as I lay swallowed in the jumper you left behind.
Your scent stained deep within the fabric, immersed only in thoughts of you.

And like a hurricane you have devastated me.
The aftermath now merely a memory.
Satisfied only by my ability to fantasize behind closed eyes.

And I wait, desperate to be with you again.

– Jessica Elaine

As I close my eyes I am balancing between fantasy and reality.
Confined to mere moments to indulge in you.

And lust burns fiercely within me causing an endless desire to be ravished by you.
Uncontrollable warmth surges throughout my body as I continue to feel the heat of your touch against my skin despite your absence.

And when alone, it is only you consuming my thoughts.
Life now permanently stained by your presence and my mind constantly exhausted.

And I am hypnotically bound to you.

– Jessica Elaine

You have pained me.
Your inability to understand consciousness.

And to touch me so recklessly, leaving my body vulnerable.
Your strength branded upon me, I was defenceless.

And I attempt to comprehend how a lifeless body is appealing.
Struggling to find words to convey the silent pain you have inflicted.

And I am left with an invisible scar against my soul from a careless night.
Discarded, my innocence now tarnished.

– Jessica Elaine

In one night, you fell so far from the pedestal on which
I had placed you.
I was enchanted by you.

And like so many before, I realize that you are nothing more
than a shadow of the person I was captivated by.
And my heart aches because it never crossed my mind, not
for a second, that you were capable of inducing such pain.

And I let you.
Because I didn't think I was worthy of your time and now I
know that I am not worthy of your respect either.

— Jessica Elaine

He has consumed my thoughts, I am absorbing every word.
He has infected me.

And I have never met anyone like him before.
And I am intimidated by his presence and his perception of life.

And I long to feel the weight of him against me. And embrace his body, taking it in against my touch.
His scent staining my skin.
And to taste him.

He has all of my attention.
And I am addicted to him.

— Jessica Elaine

And from within, I was awakened.
As though you had found me when I was lost.
And I fell in love with you so intensely that my soul was entangled within yours.

And when I awake beside you, I am overcome with the realization that without you there would be no purpose.
And my life holds purpose because you are the foundation in which I grow.

And when I hold you, I am holding everything that is of value to me.

You opened my eyes to a life I could never fathom.
I do not remember my life without you.

With you I love and I am loved.
And when you forget, I will remind you that it is always you.

– Jessica Elaine

You were an invasion on my thoughts.
My mind restricted to only you.

And lust courses throughout, suffocating me when I am alone.
A dull burn constantly residing beneath the surface.

My patience is stretched as I am reduced to fantasies formed by the sound of your voice.
And I attempt to drown in the world around me but remain permanently distracted by you.

Waiting for you is a form of punishment I no longer desire to feel.
And I unwisely hold onto the concept of hope.

– Jessica Elaine

I fell in love with you twice.

At first it was instant, surface love.
The intense colour of your eyes.

The second time held depth.
Where I could see in your eyes detachment from the world
when your mind resided elsewhere.

– Jessica Elaine

A painstakingly bleak path I have embarked on to erase you.
Attempting to close off to someone who elicits perfection into existence.

And I continue longing for a day where my face is unstained from tears cried over you.
And where thoughts are not painful but indulgent.
You occupy an untouched space within, now abandoned.

And as you dispose of me, I withdraw from the surrounding world.
And to discredit my suffering would be to deny myself the truth, that you simply are not someone I want to forget.

— Jessica Elaine

You are what I crave to experience.
Parts that confuse me and the pieces you consider are not deserving of love.

And in the privilege of your presence I am absorbing you.
The sound of your breath in rest, the depth of it as you plunge into sleep.
Mannerisms unique only to you.

And when you speak I am listening, captivated by your resilience.
Retaining the narrative that you have placed upon my ears, free from judgement.

You are complicated, but intentional.
And I would not want you any other way.

– Jessica Elaine

It is the simplicity of your touch, inducing a slow burn within.
My body responding only this way to you.

Intruding on my thoughts.
And in your absence my mind suffocates, replaying the hours I have indulged in you.
Your presence lingering as I instinctively reach out.

And I realize, you have become my subconscious investment.
For there is no contingency.
And I am left drunk on your words, hungover by your taste.

– Jessica Elaine

It is the silent pain you never witnessed, the tears I have drowned in over you.

And a time once existed when there was no hesitation to bleed for you.
And when you were the content that consumed countless pages of my mind.

But a perception of my value was exposed through your eyes.
And I felt it a privilege in your presence yet my time appeared to be of no worth.
I let you have me, an infection now remaining within my thoughts.

And in an attempt to purge you from my life,
my mind remains stolen by your voice and the memories you discarded.

– Jessica Elaine

But how can I live without you?

For my heart beats alongside yours every moment on this journey.
Within you I have found a place where my soul belongs.

The foundation that lay in the years behind us has shown that our love reaches forward.
And I will forever reach forward, with you, for you.

Still, after all these years our hands remain entwined.
And if you get lost, I will find you.
And when a storm emerges, I will clear the skies.

Challenged by the uncertainty of what tomorrow will bring, but knowing that at the end of the day you are there brings comfort to my soul.

My life is enriched with your love.

You are all that I know, you are all that I need.
Love me, not because I cannot live without you but because I do not want to.

– Jessica Elaine

Unwanted, I dreamt of you again.
A reminder of your distant existence, the unhealed internal suffering looming beneath the surface.

And in the darkness of night, I drown between the bedsheets.
A metaphor of how I spent time immersing myself completely in you.
Now deprived from your touch and my mind collapsing under a recollection of memories.

And I awake, incapable of rising.
Aware that you have burdened my subconscious as I relapse into dangerous thoughts.

— Jessica Elaine

She is suffering but you cannot help her.
She has come to the threshold of life.

The end began with her naked body sitting on the bathroom tiles, cold.
An invitation of light shines through the small window above the porcelain bathtub; almost tempting as it glistens against the white tub and light blue walls.

It was as if the light was seducing her into its warmth, it's freedom.
She breathed in with purpose, as the depths of her mind wandered without control; of how she had gotten to this point.
A naked body sat.

She peered over her body repulsed by every inch.
She hated her skin; the feeling, the colour.
She hated the lines that ran over the inside of her hands and the bottoms of her feet; hating herself for as long as she could remember.

It was hard to look in a mirror, even a reflection.
And what appeared in that reflection was invisible chains consuming her wrists, her ankles and securely tightened round her throat.
The lock binding the chains are unable to be loosened as her mind forces them in place.

Unable to glimpse at the body she was to leave behind she sits in the empty bathtub, knees curled up to her chest, a

posture of loneliness.
Tears run down her face; however she isn't crying.

An emptiness consumes her mind and what lingers are faint noises of birds amongst the trees, the distant laughter of children at the adjacent park and the wind ever so gently carrying her name,
as if it were calling her, freeing her from the torment of her existence.

Hot water, almost unbearable, begins slowly consuming the space around her.
An eerie feeling of relief devours her mind;
that all the suffering she had endured would finally cease and contentment would become her.

Eyes closed in anguish, her head now under.
Echoing sounds the water produces in her ears as her breath becomes shorter.
She thinks she hears a scream, could it be that someone cares?
Don't be absurd, no one is there.

She is drowning. Not fast, but slow.
Feeling everything around her disappear.
She is free.

– Jessica Elaine

Because you once existed in my life intimately, does not allow you to freely touch me. And you thought the lingering hand on the small of my exposed back went unnoticed. The dress was not an invitation for you.

Your hands became more arrogant as the number of drinks increased and your conscious mind slipped.
Words fell carelessly from the mouth I once lingered on, now distasteful.
Shattering my confidence before, the break within re-emerging.

And to have such poor judgement in you leaves a feeling of vulnerability to my experiences unwritten.
And I consider that this is in fact the reason why you reside in the pages of my past.

– Jessica Elaine

Fantasy and reality collide, if only for a moment.
And the space you unknowingly consume within me pleads to be relieved as my body involuntarily demands you.

And my eyes selfishly devour you as I am thrust to the border of my limit. But when exhaustion is reached, instantly I am reignited by your touch.

And in darkness I listen intently to the soundtrack of your breath as you ease into sleep.
And I speak through my hands what my voice cannot say, the nights beside you become sleepless as I blindly caress my perception of perfection.

And I reach out as you leave, desiring a moment more of intoxication.
And I attempt to fill the void that lingers in your absence, as my mind submerges in fantasy, waiting patiently for your return.

– Jessica Elaine

It was as though you were my blessing from what I had
endured in a past life.
And the universe sent you and I was to embark on a journey
I had not previously experienced.

And you give me strength and you love me when I cannot
love myself.
And with you, I am nothing more than myself.

My life is enriched through our experiences.
But being with you is the greatest adventure I have had.
Finally, I am whole.

Without question, I will always choose you.
And I am in love with my best friend.

– Jessica Elaine

Her confidence has all but diminished.
Clutching to fading thoughts that she is worth more than a single night of pleasure. An exhausted mind desiring to be ravished with love, not sex.

And she spews passion from her touch, but it is not reciprocated.
And he disposes of her body as she lingers on empty hope, hope she desperately grasps because it is more comforting than the thoughts that invade, isolating her night after night.
And she cannot remember the last time she was loved for her mind, not her body.

Internally she is burnt out from the repetition.
And as time moves forward her self-reflection flickers between person and object.
And she cries alongside the still of night, accepting that she will be nothing more than the halfway girl.

– Jessica Elaine

I wonder if others observe you as I do.
Beneath the surface, into your layers.
And I wonder if they hang on your every word, captivated
by the life you have lived.

I wonder if they have taken for granted the privilege of your
touch.
And the noting of how your skin reacts involuntarily to
fingertips, dependent on pressure.
Or if when you leave, they remain intoxicated by the linen
that wrapped your body throughout the night.

And I wonder if you are aware that my attention is confined
to you.

– Jessica Elaine